SCOTT FORESMAN
SiDEWALKS

P9-DDH-822

Changes

Program Authors

Connie Juel, Ph.D.

Jeanne R. Paratore, Ed.D.

Deborah Simmons, Ph.D.

Sharon Vaughn, Ph.D.

PEARSON
Scott
Foresman

ISBN: 0-328-21428-0

3 4 5 6 7 8 9 10 V003 12 11 10 09 08 07 06

Editorial Offices: Glenview, Illinois • Parsippany, New Jersey • New York, New York
Sales Offices: Boston, Massachusetts • Duluth, Georgia • Glenview, Illinois
Coppell, Texas • Sacramento, California • Mesa, Arizona

UNIT 3 Contents

Changes

Growing and Changing

SiDEWALKS

Changes in Nature

Contents

Growing and Changing

See page 29 for My New Words and Pictionary!

Let's Find Out

We All Grow

Look at the little duck.

It was in a shell.

The little duck is not big yet.
But its mom and dad are big now.

Little duck will get just as big.

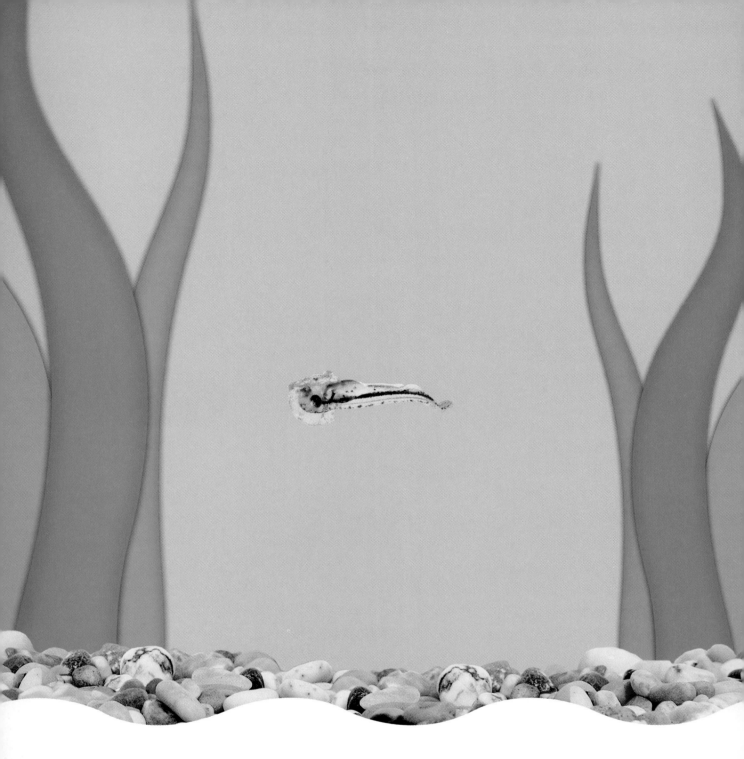

Look at the little fish.
Where are its fins?

It will get fins. It will get big.
Big fish use fins to swim.

Look at Trish. Trish is still little.
Trish can not stand up yet.

But Trish will get big.
Trish will get big like her mom.

Little Duck

by Patricia Wydell

An egg jumps in a nest.
Tap! Tap!
What is in this egg?

The thin shell cracks.
It is a little duck.

Duck can not sit up yet.
Sh! Rest now, Duck.

Plop! Plop! The ducks jump in a pond.
Can Duck swim with them? Yes.
Duck can use her legs to swim.

Duck hunts for fresh bugs and plants.
Quack! Quack! Yum! Yum!

Duck will get big fast.
Just look at her now!

Big

and
Small

by Pete Hill

illustrated by
Luciana Navarro Alves

Josh is big. Josh is six.
Beth is small. Beth is just one.

Can Beth walk? A little bit.

She still falls a lot.

Josh helps her walk.

Can Beth talk? A little bit.

Beth can call Josh.

Then Josh grins at her.

Can Beth use her blocks? A little bit.

Her blocks fall.

Josh helps her use them.

Can Beth swim? Not now.

Can Josh swim? Yes!
Josh can swim like a fish.

Will Beth get big? Yes!
Then Beth will walk and talk.

Beth will use her blocks.
Beth will swim with Josh.

SECRET

Read Together

by Beverly McLoughland

Mrs. Kangaroo,

Is it true,

Are you hiding

Someone new

In the pocket

Part of you?

There must be someone

New and growing,

His little ears

Have started showing.

My New Words

her   We have **her** book.
Give **her** this book.

now   Take the dog out **now**.

use   You **use** an umbrella to
stay dry.

Pictionary

grin

 pond

Contents

Growing and Changing

See page 53 for My New Words and Pictionary!

Learning New Things

Little kids can not do a lot.
Kids must get help.
Moms and dads must help them.

Kids get big.

But kids can make a mess.

Kids want moms and dads to help.

Kids get big.

Big kids can do a lot.

But moms and dads can still help.

Moms and dads want to make all kids safe.

Now the same kids are old.

The same kids are moms and dads.

They can help kids too.

Kids Can Do Lots

by Kim Lee

Swish!

In grade 1, kids are not too old.
But kids can do lots.
What can you do?

In grade 1, kids like fun games.
Kids can make faces. Look at
that face! Can you make faces?

In grade 1, kids can skate.
Kids can skate from place to place.

Zoom!

Kids want to race and skate fast.
Can you skate?

In grade 1, kids can hit balls.
Kids can hit them past bases.
Can you hit balls?

In grade 1, kids can do lots.
What can you do?

Jake
and the
Surprise

by Daniel Ortiz
illustrated by Barry Gott

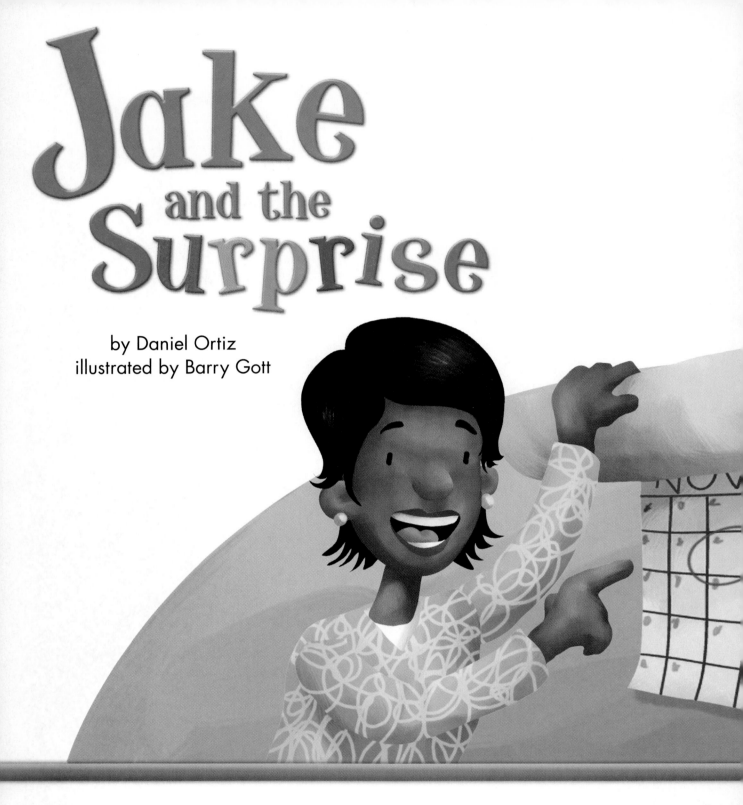

"Look at this page," said Mom.

Dad did.

"Jake is age six on that date," said
Mom. "We can get Jake gifts."

"Yes, but what will Jake want?"
said Dad.

Just then, Jake came in.

Mom had to spell the gifts that
she will get.

"P-e-t-s in a c-a-g-e," said Mom.

But Jake gave mom and dad a surprise too.

"Mom and Dad, I am in grade 1," said Jake. "I am old and big."

"Yes," said Mom and Dad.

"And I can s-p-e-l-l *pets* and *cage*," said Jake.

Dad had a big grin on his face.

"You are not too old for big, big h-u-g-s," said Mom.

"Not yet," said Jake.

And that is just what Mom
gave him!

This Is the Way We Sing a Song

This is the way we brush our teeth,
Brush our teeth, brush our teeth.
This is the way we brush our teeth,
So early in the morning.

This is the way we brush our hair . . .
This is the way we read a book . . .
This is the way we sing a song . . .

What else do you do in the morning?

My New Words

old   The **old** wall has a crack.
Jake is six years **old**.

too   She can run and jump **too**.
She can not run **too** fast.

want   The kids **want** a big snack.

Pictionary

gift

surprise

Contents

Growing and Changing

See page 79 for My New Words and Pictionary!

Exciting Changes

There are big, big days in your life.

If you get five black and tan pups,
it is a big, big day.
Will all five pups like you?

If you ride a big, big bike,
it is a big, big day.

Who will smile and brag with pride?

If a van takes you from place to place, it is a big, big day.

Will you miss best pals?
Yes, but you will make new pals.

Kids will get big.

Kids will pass from grade to grade.

Kids will take fun trips.
Kids will have big, big days!

In the Crib

by Craig Stevens • illustrated by Mary Collier

Who rests in that white crib?
This baby rests there.
He wants Mom and Dad all the time.

When will you get time with them?

While Baby rests, Mom and Dad
hush you.

Did Mom and Dad hush kids while
you slept?
Yes, Mom and Dad did.

When Baby wakes up, Mom and
Dad spend lots of time with him.

Did they spend time with you?
Yes, Mom and Dad did.

Baby makes Mom and Dad smile.

Did Mom and Dad smile a lot at you?
Yes, and your mom and dad still do!

A New Kid

by Olga Kersta
illustrated by
Jackie Snider

There is a new kid who will come
to this class. Sam is the new kid.

"What is Sam like? When will he get here?" That is what we kept asking.

Chuck kept asking, "Can Sam catch? Can Sam pitch?"

Rich kept asking, "Can Sam ride a bike fast? Can he ice skate?"

Mike kept asking, "Can Sam run fast?
Can Sam chase and catch us in tag?"

Then the new kid came to class.
But Sam was not a "he."

"Sam is in your class," said Miss Chen.
"Sam can bat, pitch, ride a bike,
skate, run fast, and catch you in tag."

"Sam is grand!" said Chuck and
Rich and Mike. "Come pitch and hit
with us!"

Here Comes the School Bus

Maple Street

Lake Street

Elm Street

School Street

Main Street

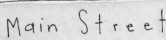

Use your finger to show
how the bus gets to school.

How do you get to school?

78

My New Words

there **There** are 12 houses on our block.

who **Who** is at the door?

your Tell me about **your** dream.

Pictionary

baby

new

pitch

Contents

Changes in Nature

See page 107 for My New Words and Pictionary!

How Does a Garden Change?

winter

The pond froze.
This garden was just a big
patch of ice.

Plants could not poke up in
the ice, not yet.

spring

Then ice gets thin and melts.
Wet drops fall and fall on
the garden.

Grass gets very green and tall.
Buds pop up on stems of garden
plants.

summer

Next the sun is hot.
Gardens fill with red and
yellow roses.

Can your nose smell these roses?

Mine can.

Bugs buzz and eat bits of plants.

fall

Then winds chill gardens.
Winds nip your nose.

Buds close, and roses fall.

Ice will be back.

Plants get set to rest.

BUGS!

by Lin Chen

Stop and look at gardens.
You'll spot bugs, lots and lots of them.

Bugs buzz past your nose!
Bugs walk on plants and stones.

Green Stink Bug

But you can't spot all bugs.
Small bugs can hide very well.

Walking Stick Bug

Praying Mantis

And bugs can look like stems and sticks.

Grasshopper

Aphids

Bad bugs don't help gardens.
Bad bugs eat stems and
buds and vines.

Japanese Beetle

Bad bugs could eat too much!
Bad bugs can kill plants.

Ladybug

But bugs can help gardens too.
They'll eat bad plants and bad bugs.

Butterfly

Bumblebee

Bugs can help plants get big.
All gardens can use bugs that help!

Worms Help Plants

by Sonia Muñoz
illustrated by Jason Wolff

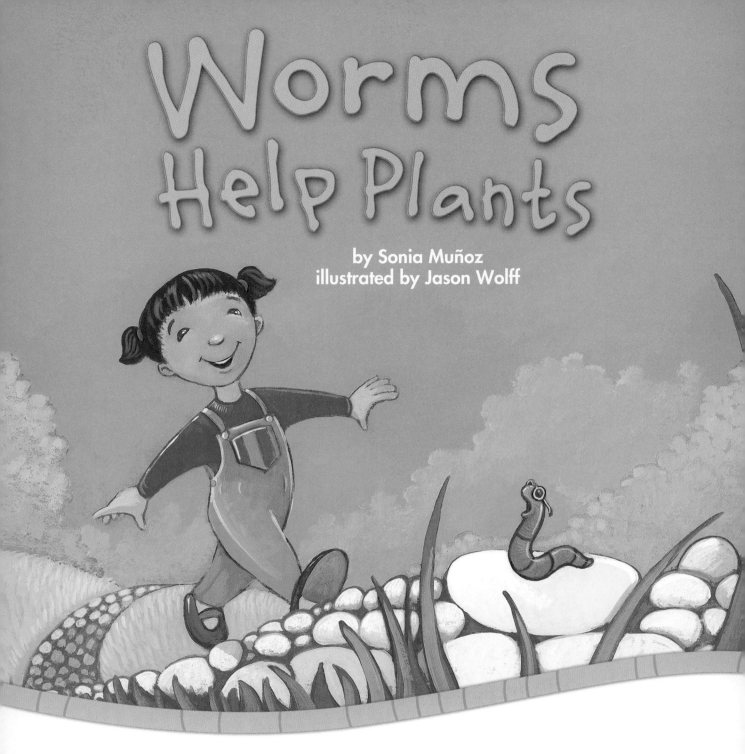

Yikes, Kid! Do not step on this white stone! You could step on me. And if you step on me, it'll make plants very sad!

98

Yes, I'm just a small worm!
But worms help make nice dirt.
Plants like that. And plants like us.

Dirt is the place I call home.

I do not like it when that home is wet.

If it is wet, I rest on stones and rocks.

If dirt isn't wet, I slide back in it.

Plant bits fall in dirt.

I will munch and munch on them.

And I will eat bits of bugs!

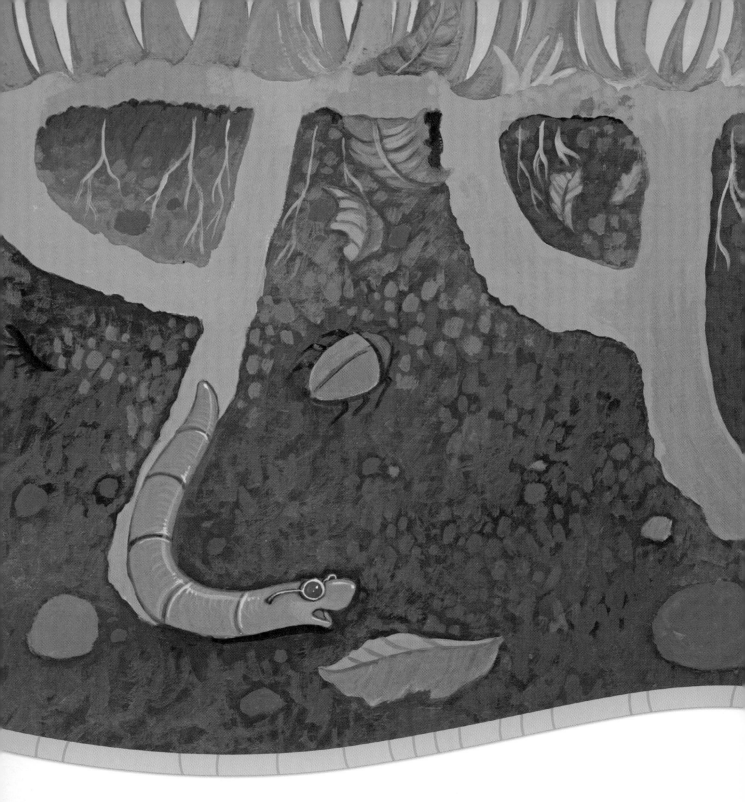

While I munch, I dig small
holes in the dirt.
I dig lots and lots of small holes.

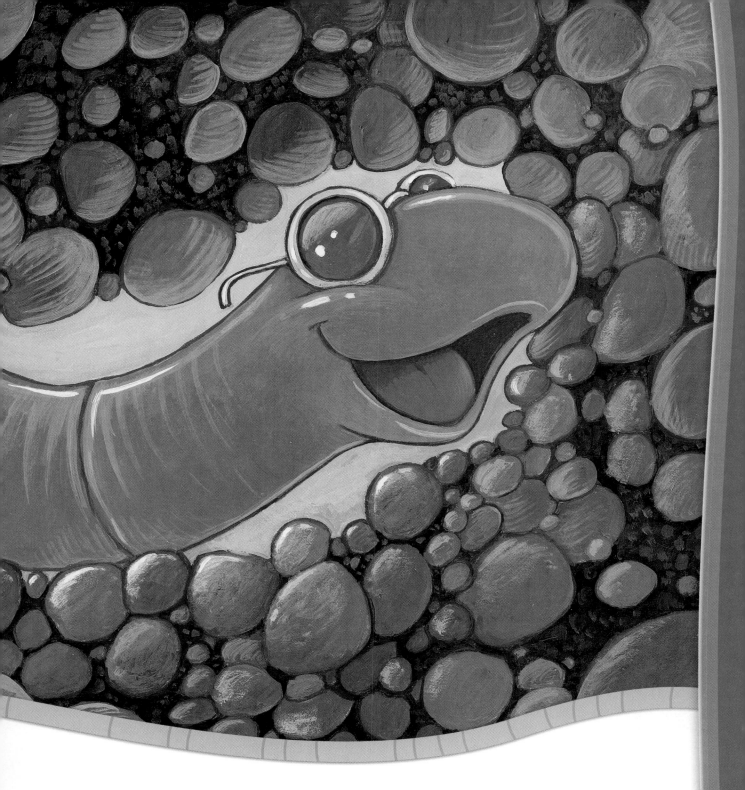

Those small holes make nice dirt!
And all those holes help plants.

You can see that plants like me.
Worms can make nice dirt.
That helps plants get big and tall.

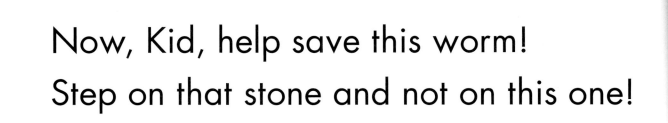

Now, Kid, help save this worm!
Step on that stone and not on this one!

Plant Parts

flower

leaf

leaf

stem

stem

root

roots

Name the parts
of the plants.
Which can you eat?

106

My New Words

could   She **could** jump well.

eat   When you **eat**, you chew and swallow food.

very   July was **very** hot this year.

Pictionary

dirt

garden

worm

Contents

Changes in Nature

See page 129 for My New Words and Pictionary!

Watch What Changes

A small white egg rests on a plant.
When will this small white egg hatch?
And what will pop out?

110

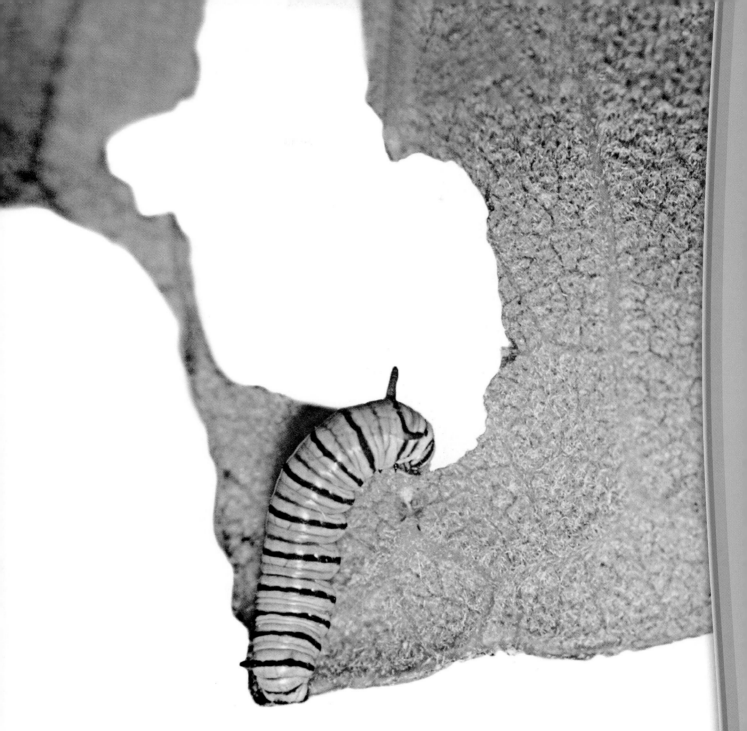

That white egg we saw did hatch.
This small caterpillar came out.
This small caterpillar eats lots and lots.

Take a good look at this caterpillar.
It makes its shell on this twig.

What is next?
What will it use this shell for?

At last, it sheds its shell.

What is it?

It is a nice big butterfly.

It is a huge butterfly!

The Same

by Alison Laine

Can we see snakes change?
This snake will shed its old skin.

It will get fresh skin.
But it is still the same snake.

Can we see this crab change?
Crabs need good shells.
They can use shells left out on the sand.

This crab seems like the same crab we just saw.

It is. This is the same crab with a good shell!

This bug changes a lot.
It is small.
Then it gets big.

See it in the tree? It is big and green.

Snakes, crabs, and bugs can change.
But they are still the same.

What Am I?

by Lee Tsang

illustrated by Don Tate

Out on a tree branch sits Fuzz.

Fuzz seems just like a cute worm.

But she keeps asking, "What am I?"

This is Tad.

Tad swims in Green Pond.

Tad swims just like a good fish.

But he keeps asking, "What am I?"

Fuzz sees Tad in Green Pond.
"Am I a worm?" Fuzz asks.

"Yes!" yells Tad. "Am I a fish?"

"Yes!" yells Fuzz.

Then Fuzz hides in an odd shell.
She can't see Tad.

Tad can't spot the worm he saw.

Next, Tad feels big changes.

He has legs! He has feet! He can walk!

Then Fuzz gets free from her shell.
"I am a butterfly," she yells and smiles.

And Tad hops from pad to pad.
"I am a frog," he yells and smiles.

A Frog's Life

A frog starts as an egg.

A tadpole hatches.

Back legs grow.

Front legs grow.

Look! It's a frog!

My New Words

good   A **good** person or animal is kind and behaves well.

out   We went **out** the door. The lights went **out**.

saw   She **saw** a bird yesterday.

Pictionary

butterfly

caterpillar

Contents

Changes in Nature

See page 157 for My New Words and Pictionary!

Let's Find Out

When Seasons Change

Hot, hot weeks are here!
Yellow sun shines down.

Tall trees are dressed in green.
Bees seem to buzz with life and fun.

Hot weeks have passed.
Trees are dressed in red and yellow.

Plants and bugs feel a big chill
on the way.

Winter hides sleeping plants and grass.
Ice bends tall trees.

Ponds freeze and kids skate.
This chill will not last.

The ice has melted now.
Hot sun is back at work.

Green buds have filled the trees.
Chicks peep and plants get tall.

Winter Changes

by David Elliot

Will this rabbit look the same all the time?
Last winter this rabbit was white.
That helped it hide.

140

Now it is not white.
Can it still hide?

Lakes freeze in winter.
Ducks go to a hot place.

But ducks come back when winter has passed.

This animal will take a big nap. It will sleep all winter.

It is hidden deep down in this cave.
What will happen if we wake it up?

This small animal can't get nuts in winter. It must work and save nuts now.

This way it can still munch on nuts all winter.

What Time Is Best?

by Maria Polomarkaki   illustrated by Maribel Suarez

What time is best? Is it summer?

Is it fall? Is it winter?

Is it spring? Let me see.

Last summer, we ran in the sand.
We dashed with kites. Zip!
We hid. Hide and seek! Peek!
I like summer.

Last fall, Dennis passed me the ball.
I passed it back in a flash.

We had on thick plastic helmets.
We crashed. Crack!
We ran fast and had fun. I like fall.

Last winter, Ellen and I rode sleds.
We walked up big hills.
Thump! Thump! That felt like work!

We yelled and dashed down
those big hills. I like winter.

Last spring, Dad and Mom walked with
me way up on Blossom Hill.
We had a lunch basket. Keep out, ants!
We had a nice picnic. I like spring.

What time is best? Is it summer?
Is it fall? Is it winter? Is it spring?
I can't tell. I like them all.

Did You Know?

June 21 is the longest day of the year. It is the first day of summer.

December 21 is the shortest day of the year. It is the first day of winter.

In the winter, the North Pole has long dark days. In the summer, the North Pole has long light days.

North Pole

My New Words

down When you go **down**, you go to a lower place.

way A **way** is how something is done.
A **way** is also the path you follow to get to a place.

work When you **work**, you do your job.

Pictionary

animals

melt

Acknowledgments

Poetry

28 "Secret" by Beverly McLoughland. Reprinted by permission of the author.

Illustrations

5, 28 Ariel Pang; **26** Luciana Navarro Alves; **30, 45–50** Barry Gott; **46–49** John Wallace; **52** Keiko Motoyama; **55, 78** Steven Mach; **64–66, 68–69** Mary Collier; **70, 72–76** Jackie Snider; **98–105** Jason Wolff; **106** Linda Holt Ayriss; **109, 128** Kathy Wilburn; **122–127** Don Tate; **130, 148, 150, 152, 154; 155** Maribel Suarez; **156** Chris Lensch

Photographs

Every effort has been made to secure permission and provide appropriate credit for photographic material. The publisher deeply regrets any omission and pledges to correct errors called to its attention in subsequent editions.

Unless otherwise acknowledged, all photographs are the property of Scott Foresman, a division of Pearson Education.

Photo locators denoted as follows: Top (T), Center (C), Bottom (B), Left (L), Right (R), Background (Bkgd).

5 Getty Images; **6** Barrie Watts/© DK Images; **7** Barrie Watts/© DK Images; **8** Jane Burton/© DK Images; **9** Steve Shott/© DK Images; **10** (B) Max Gibbs/© DK Images, (C) Neil Fletcher/© DK Images; **11** Max Gibbs/© DK Images; **12** © Jo Ford/© DK Images; **13** © RubberBall/SuperStock; **14** (T) Getty Images, (C) Barrie Watts/© DK Images, (CR) Siede Preis/Getty Images; **15** Barrie Watts/© DK Images; **16** Jane Burton/© DK Images; **17** © Mary Rhodes/Animals Animals/Earth Scenes; **18** Barrie Watts/© DK Images; **19** Barrie Watts/© DK Images; **29** (C) Getty Images, (BC) © Gail Shumway/Getty Images; **31** © Steve Satushek/Getty Images; **32** (BR) © Ken Huang/Getty Images, (CL) © Zave Smith/Corbis; **34** © Buccina Studios/Getty Images; **36** © Royalty–Free/Corbis; **37** © Jose Luis Pelaez/Corbis; **38** (TR) © Steve Satushek/Getty Images, (CL) © Brand X Pictures/Getty Images, (CR) Getty Images; **40** © John Terence Turner/Getty Images; **41** © Richard Hamilton Smith/Corbis; **42** (CR) © George Shelley/Corbis, (CL) © Brand X Pictures/Getty Images; **43** (BL) © Brand X Pictures/Getty Images, (TR) © John Terence Turner/Getty Images; **53** (BR) © Rubberball Productions/Getty Images, (C) © Myrleen Ferguson Cate/PhotoEdit; **55** © SuperStock/Alamy Images; **56** © Jim Craigmyle/Corbis; **57** © Paul Barton/Corbis; **58** © SuperStock/Alamy Images; **60** © Superstock/Alamy Images; **61** © Ariel Skelley/Masterfile Corporation; **62** (CL) © Paul Barton/Corbis, (C) © Ron Chapple/Getty Images; **63** (TL) © BananaStock/Alamy Images, (CR) © Michelle Pedone/Photonica/Getty Images; **67** Getty Images; **79** (C) © C Squared Studios/Photodisc/Getty Images, (BC) © Duomo/Corbis; **81** © Burke/Triolo/Brand X Pictures; **82** © Hiroyuki Matsumoto/Getty Images; **83** © Photodisc/Getty Images; **84** (C) © Gary Buss/Taxi/Getty Images, (BR) © C Squared Studios/Getty Images; **85** (C) Getty Images, (BL) © Botanica/Jupiter Images; **86** © Tim Street–Porter/Botanica/Getty Images; **87** (C) © Mark E. Gibson Stock Photography, (BL) © J Luke/PhotoLink/Getty Images; **88** (BR) © Siede Preis/Getty Images, (C) © Stone/Getty Images; **89** © Ron Evans/Garden Picture Library; **90** (C) © Leroy Simon/Visuals Unlimited, (CL) © DK Images, (CR) © GK Hart/Vikki Hart/Getty Images, (BR) Getty Images; **91** © Steve Satushek/Getty Images; **92** © Breck P. Kent/Animals Animals/Earth Scenes; **93** (T) © GK Hart/Vikki Hart/Getty Images, (CL) © Scott W. Smith/Animals Animals/Earth Scenes; **94** (CL) Neil Fletcher/© DK Images, (TR) © George Grall/National Geographic Image Collection; **95** © David Caton/Alamy; **97** (TL) © George Grall/Getty Images, (BR) © DK Images; **107** (BR) Brand X Pictures, (CL, BL) © DK Images; **109** © Breck P. Kent/Animals Animals/Earth Scenes; **110** © Dick Poe/Visuals Unlimited; **111** © Bill Beatty/Visuals Unlimited; **112** © Richard Walters/Visuals Unlimited; **113** © David Cavagnaro/Visuals Unlimited; **114** Getty Images; **115** Photodisc Red/Getty Images; **116** © Zigmund Leszczynski/Animals Animals/Earth Scenes; **117** © Breck P. Kent/Animals Animals/Earth Scenes; **118** (CL, C) Getty Images, (T) Frank Greenaway/© DK Images; **119** © DK Images; **120** (TL, CR) Pennsylvania Department of Conservation & Natural Resources, (C) © Bill Beatty/Visuals Unlimited; **129** (C) © MedioImages/Getty Images, (BR) Getty Images; **132** © Masterfile Royalty–Free; **133** © Profimedia.CZ s.r.o./Alamy Images; **134** Getty Images; **135** © The Image Bank/Getty Images; **136** © Luc Struyf/The Image Bank/Getty Images; **137** © LWA/The Image Bank/Getty Images; **138** © Digital Archive Japan/Alamy; **139** © Photodisc/Getty Images; **141** Photodisc Green/Getty Images; **142** © Reino Hanninen/Alamy Images; **143** © Pal Hermansen/Getty Images; **144** © Tom J. Ulrich/Visuals Unlimited; **145** Photodisc Green/Getty Images; **146** © Dianna Sarto/Corbis; **147** © Robert W. Ginn/Alamy Images; **157** (CL) Photodisc Blue/Getty Images, (BR) Getty Images, (TC, BC, BL) © GK Hart/Vikki Hart/Getty Images